Wild Britain

Towns and Cities

Louise and Richard Spilsbury

Heinemann
LIBRARY

www.heinemann.co.uk
Visit our website to find out more information about Heinemann Library books.

To order:
☎ Phone 44 (0) 1865 888066
📄 Send a fax to 44 (0) 1865 314091
💻 Visit the Heinemann Bookshop at www.heinemann.co.uk to browse our catalogue and order online.

First published in Great Britain by Heinemann Library, Halley Court, Jordan Hill, Oxford OX2 8EJ, part of Harcourt Education Ltd. Heinemann is a registered trademark of Harcourt Education Ltd.

Editorial: Lucy Thunder and Helen Cox
Design: David Poole and Celia Floyd
Illustrations: Alan Fraser and Geoff Ward
Picture Research: Catherine Bevan and Peter Morris
Production: Sevy Ribierre

Originated by Dot Gradations
Printed and bound in Hong Kong, China by South China Printing

ISBN 0 431 03921 6 (hardback)
07 06 05 04 03
10 9 8 7 6 5 4 3 2 1

ISBN 0 431 03926 7 (paperback)
08 07 06 05 04
10 9 8 7 6 5 4 3 2 1

British Library Cataloguing in Publication Data
Spilsbury, Louise and Spilsbury, Richard
Towns and cities. – (Wild Britain)
577.5'6'0941
A full catalogue record for this book is available from the British Library.

Acknowledgements

The Publishers would like to thank the following for permission to reproduce photographs: Bruce Coleman pp9 (Janos Jurka), 24, 25 (Kim Taylor), Corbis pp4 (Karen Huntt Mason), 16 (Hubert Stadler), 21 (Robert Pickett), 23 (Jonathan Blair); Ecoscene p29 (Chinch Gryniewicz); FLPA pp10 (H Clark), 11 (E & D Hosking), 17 (A R Hamblin), 18 (Derek A Robinson) 20 (H B Casals), 26 (T Whittaker), 27 (R Tidman); Peter Morris pp5, 6, 12, 13, 14, 15, 28; Rex Features p22; Science Photo Library pp8 (BSIP Chassenet), 19 (Pascal Goetgheluck); Still Pictures p7 (Piet Munsterman).

Cover photograph of Large Bindweed with tower blocks in London, reproduced with permission of NHPA (David Woodfall).

The publishers would like to thank Michael Scott for his assistance in the preparation of this book.

Every effort has been made to contact copyright holders of any material reproduced in this book. Any omissions will be rectified in subsequent printings if notice is given to the Publisher.

Contents

Any words appearing in the text in bold, **like this**, are explained in the Glossary.

What are towns and cities?

In towns and cities there are many buildings, and roads with lots of traffic.

We all know what towns and cities are – many of us live in one! Towns and cities are places where people live and work.

Plants and animals find many different places to live and things to eat in towns and cities.

Plants and animals also live in towns and cities. A **habitat** is a place where a group of plants and animals live. In this book we will look at some of the plants and animals that live in town and city habitats.

Town and city habitats

These wild plants are growing in a churchyard.

Plants and animals live in parks, gardens and in other places in a city, too. Plants grow on walls, streets and buildings. Animals also live in churchyards, playing fields and in roofs or buildings.

This fox lives near a railway line.

Animals often live by railway lines or around canals. These are quiet places where not many people go. Animals can travel safely along these quiet pathways.

Changes

People living in a city often find wasps and bees a nuisance in summer.

Spring and summer are warm **seasons**. Many **insects**, like bees and butterflies, feed in streets and gardens. They drink **nectar** from spring flowers.

Herring gulls come from cliffs to spend winter in the city. They rest on roofs and eat food dropped by people.

In winter, insects rest underground to avoid the cold. Many birds stay in cities or visit them in winter. City buildings are warm and their walls give **shelter** from wind.

Living there

This Pipistrelle bat rests in a roof in the daytime and goes out to feed at night.

Towns and cities are built on land that was once wild, such as woodland. Animals that lived in the wild had to find new homes. Bats that lived in trees now live in roofs!

This grey squirrel is looking for food in a bin.

Some animals live in towns and cities because it is easy for them to find food. Hedgehogs feed on the snails that like to live near walls. Rats, squirrels and foxes eat waste food from bins or off the roads.

Wasteland wildlife

The first plants to grow on wasteland are tough. They can grow well even in a thin layer of soil.

When land is left alone, plants soon begin to grow there. **Seeds** blow on to the **soil** and start to grow. Daisies, dandelions and nettles often grow on **wasteland**.

The land by this railway line is overgrown with plants. There are lots of places for animals to hide.

Insects soon begin to visit the area to feed on the plants. Birds come to eat the insects. Birds also make **nests** among the bigger plants that grow on wasteland.

Streets and pavements

Only tough plants like this dandelion can live in a busy street where they are trodden on.

City streets may look empty of wildlife, but it is there if you look closely. Plants like grass and dandelions grow in **soil** that gathers in pavement cracks.

This snail is eating some grass on a pavement.

Small animals, such as woodlice, spiders, slugs, earthworms and snails live under paving stones or in cracks in a street. They come out to eat the plants.

Living on a wall

Ivy plants have a main root in the ground. Little roots grow out of the main stem to help it climb up a wall.

Some plants grow on city walls. Moss grows in tiny bits of **soil** between bricks. Ivy plants climb up walls. Small **roots** grow out of the ivy **stem** to hold it up.

Birds, like this blackbird, visit walls to eat ivy berries. They also make **nests** behind tangled ivy stems.

Lots of small animals live among the plants on a wall. They hide there from hungry birds. Spiders hunt for flies to eat. Earwigs, snails and woodlice hide between bricks or in cracks in the wall.

Ants

These ants are eating a piece of apple. Ants sniff out food using the **antennae** on their heads.

Ants are a kind of **insect**. They live in cities because they can eat so many different things. They eat plant parts and other insects. They also eat our food!

These ants are carrying a grain of rice back to their nest.

Groups of ants live in **nests** between pavement stones or underground. Some ants stay in the nest. Others go out to find food and bring it back to the nest to share.

Flies and cockroaches

Flies, like this bluebottle, suck up food. They do this with their long hollow tongue, called a proboscis.

Flies are **insects** that eat sweet or rotting food. Like ants, flies find food using their **antennae**. The buzzing sound flies make is the noise of their wings beating.

Cockroaches can be a problem. They can spread **germs** on to our food.

Cockroaches are insects with flat oval bodies. They are covered with bristles that they feel things with. They eat all sorts of things – food scraps, litter and even soap!

City birds

Pigeons feed together like this to be safe. If one spots an enemy, like a cat, it can warn all the others.

Pigeons often gather together in city centres. They **perch** on high buildings or trees. They eat **seeds** from trees, and also fly down to eat scraps of food dropped by people.

If you look up and see a fluttering black cloud like this, it may be a flock of starlings!

Starlings often feed and fly together in large **flocks**. In cities they build **nests** in a hole in a wall or under a roof. They fly down to the ground to find food, like **insects**, earthworms and fruit.

Night-time flyers

This barn owl is landing on a gravestone in a churchyard. It can spot small animals to eat from here.

At night it is quiet and there are few people about. Owls and bats come out to hunt. Owls **perch** on walls or street lamps to watch out for small animals, like mice.

A Pipistrelle bat like this can catch and eat up to 3000 insects a night!

Midges and many other **insects** fly around street lamps at night. Bats swoop down with open mouths to catch and eat these flying insects. Bats also eat moths.

Rats and mice

Rats have sharp, strong front teeth. They can bite through packets to get food.

Many city animals eat food that people store or throw away. Rats and mice chew holes in wooden cupboards to get the food inside. There are more rats and mice in towns than any other **mammals** – even humans!

Mice sometimes tear bits of paper to make a nest.

House mice live wherever it is dark and they can find **shelter**. They may build a **nest** in a garage roof or in an old box.

Dangers

When animals come out from roadside plants, they may be hurt by traffic.

The biggest dangers for city wildlife are people and traffic. Many animals in towns and cities are knocked down on the roads by cars.

When wasteland is cleared, animals living there have to find new homes.

Sometimes people clear areas of **wasteland**. They cut down the wild plants and put buildings on the land. Animals that lived there lose their homes.

Food chain

All plants and animals in a town or city **habitat** are connected through the food they eat. Food chains show how different living things are linked. Here is one example:

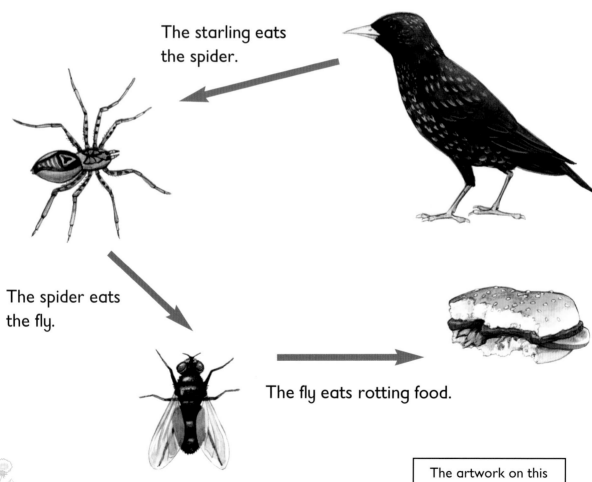

The starling eats the spider.

The spider eats the fly.

The fly eats rotting food.

The artwork on this page is not to scale.

Glossary

antennae   feelers on an insect's head used to find food

flock   group of animals feeding or living together

germs   living things so small we cannot see them. Germs can make us ill.

habitat   natural home of a group of plants or animals

insect   small animal that has six legs when an adult

mammals   group of animals that feed their babies on milk. They have hair on their bodies.

nectar   sweet, sugary juice in the centre of a flower

nest   something an animal makes to rest in or to have young in

perch   when birds sit on a branch or other object

roots   parts of a plant that grow in the soil and take in water from the soil

season   a year is divided into four seasons – spring, summer, autumn and winter

seeds   these are made by a plant and released to grow into new plants

shelter   somewhere safe to stay, live and have young

soil   also called mud or earth. Soil is made of many things, including tiny pieces of rock and rotted parts of plants.

stem   stalk that holds up the leaves and flowers of a plant

wasteland   land that people once used, but which has been left alone for a long time

Index